Conception of the project and coordination:
Violaine Bouvet-Lanselle, musée du Louvre
Gathering of the pictures and writing of the captions:
Fanny Meurisse
Collaboration: Damien Salhorgne

Publishing manager: Anne de Bouchony, Gallimard Jeunesse
Publishing coordination: Nathalie Corradini
Graphic Design: Anne-Catherine Boudet

Pictures credit: © Erich Lessing

ISBN Gallimard Jeunesse: 978-2-07-061553-7
ISBN Louvre: 978-2-35031-137-1
© Gallimard Jeunesse-Musée du Louvre, Paris, 2007
Numéro d'édition: 153095
Loi n° 46-956 du 16 juillet 1949
sur les publications destinées à la jeunesse
Dépôt légal: October 2007
Printed in China

Table of contents

Children

The Virgin and Child with the Infant Saint John the Baptist
Raphael

Master Francis George Hare
Sir Joshua Reynolds

1 The Dauphin Charles-Orlant
Master of Moulins

2 Gabrielle Arnault as a Childt
Louis-Léopold Boilly

3 A Princess
from Akhenaten Family
Egypt

9

La baronne de Krüdener and her Son
Angelika Kauffmann

Mme Vigée-Lebrun and her Daughter
Élisabeth-Louise Vigée-Lebrun

The Child with a Teetotum
Jean-Baptiste-Siméon Chardin

The Young Drawer
Jan Lievens

Grace
Jean-Baptiste-Siméon Chardin

Hélène Fourment
and Two of her Children
Petrus Paulus Rubens

Portrait of the Children of John Angerstein
Thomas Lawrence

Young Boys Playing Dice in front
of the Christiansborg Palace in Copenhagen
Constantin Hansen

Ramses II as a Child
Egypt

right hand page
Presumed Portrait of Magdalena Luther
Lucas Cranach

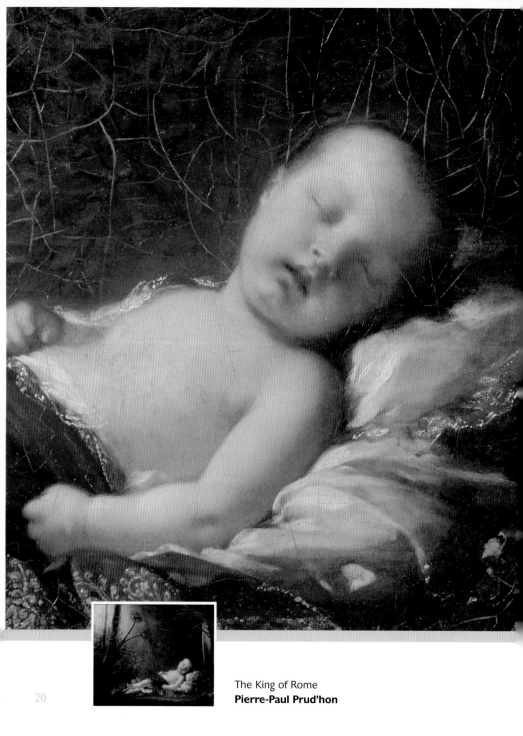

The King of Rome
Pierre-Paul Prud'hon

Alexandre Brongniart
Jean-Antoine Houdon

Louise Brongniart
Jean-Antoine Houdon

Jean-Baptiste Isabey
and his Daughter Alexandrin
François Gérard

Portrait of an Old Man and a Young Boy
Domenico Ghirlandaio

Portrait of a Youth
Parmigianino

Benoît-Agnès Trioson
Anne-Louis Girodet de Roussy-Trioson

Betchou and his Family
Egypt

The Downpour
Louis-Léopold Boilly

Everyday Life

The Peasant Family in an Interior
Antoine – or Louis – Le Nain

Chair
Egypt

Dessert with Wafer Biscuits
Lubin Baugin

Basket of Peaches, with Walnuts,
Knife and Glass of Wine
Jean-Baptiste-Siméon Chardin

previous page
The Angel's Kitchen
Bartolomé Estebán Murillo

left hand page
Madame Récamier
Jacques-Louis David

M. Levett and Mlle Giavani
in Turkish Dress
Jean-Étienne Liotard   39

Women of Algiers in their Apartment
Eugène Delacroix

Seated Nude
Christopher Wilhem Eckersberg

2

1 Model of a granary
Egypt

2 Cosmetic spoon
with girl swimming
Egypt

3 Grape harvest dish
François-Désiré Froment-Meurice

View of an Interior
Samuel Van Hoogstraten

Hyante et Climene at their Toilette
Toussaint Dubreuil

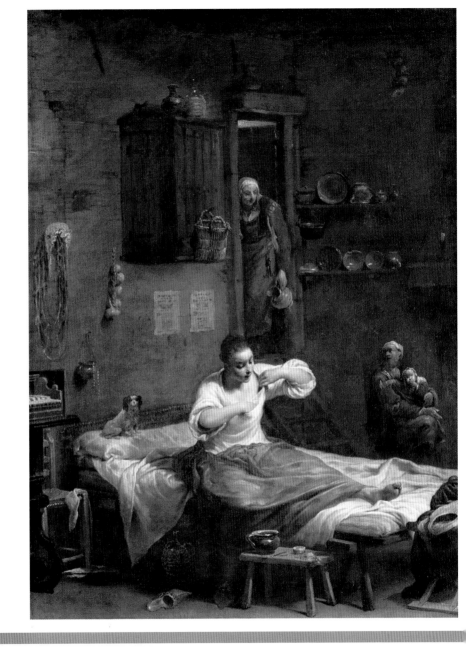

Stele of Nefertiabet
Egypt

The Lunch
François Boucher

Games and Celebrations

The Card Sharp
Georges de La Tour

previous page
Carnival Scene
Giandomenico Tiepolo

left hand page
The Wedding Feast of the Duke of Joyeuse
French School

Pierrot
Jean-Antoine Watteau

57

Walking Actor
Bald Actor
Myrina

The Guitar Player
David Teniers the Younger

Noble Children in a Chariot
Ferdinand Bol

The Game of Chess
Paris

previous page
The Marriage of Cana
Véronèse

Bell-Shaped Idol
Thebes

Winter
Nicolas Lancret

A Concert
Leonello Spada

Amon Djedkhonsoujouefankh's Musician Playing the Harp
in front of the God Re-Horakhty
Egypt

The Two Carriages
Claude Gillot

Two Figures in a Cart
Ugarit

Warriors in a Cart
Ancient Cyprus

The Ship of Fools
Hieronymus Bosch

Halt during the Hunt
Carle Vanloo

Jobs

The Moneylender and his Wife
Quentin Metsys

The Seated Scribe
Egypt

Women Carrying Offerings
Egypt

The Provider
Jean-Baptiste-Siméon Chardin

Saint Joseph Carpenter
Georges de La Tour

Cook with Mortar and Pestle
Greece

79

previous page
The Beggars
Pieter I Breughel the Elder

Saint Cecilia with an Angel Holding
Domenichino

Woman Playing the Lute
Greece

Woman Playing the Zither
Greece

La Dentellière
Johannes Vermeer

The Sharpener
David Teniers the Younger

The Fortune Teller
Nicolas Régnier

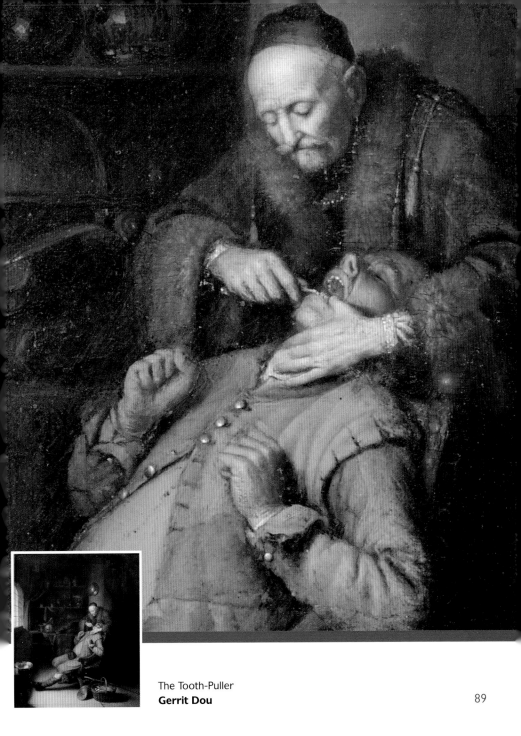

The Tooth-Puller
Gerrit Dou

Frieze of Archers
Iran

Statuette of a Peddler
Italy ?

The School-Master
Adriaen Van Ostade

The Grocer
Gerrit Dou

Model of a ploughing scene
Egypt

Ploughman
Egypt

top of the page
The Harvest
Egypt

Animals

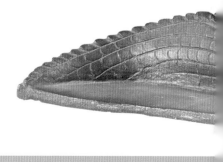

The Skate
Jean-Baptiste-Siméon Chardin

Crocodile
Egypt

Passant lion from the lion freize
Iran

2 Lion (Temple Guardian)
Syria

3 Head of Lioness
Théodore Géricault

Head of a White Horse
Théodore Géricault

Ostrich
After Giambologna

Bitch and her Pup
Greece

Dog holding a piece of cake
Greece

Cardinal Granvella's Dwarf holding a Large Dog
Antonio MORO

Goddess Bastet
Egypt

The Sideboard
Jean-Baptiste-Siméon Chardin

Hawk, vulture
Egypt

Group of Birds Perched
on Branches
Frans Snyders

Horse Held by a Groom
Guillaume Coustou

Milo of Croton
Pierre Puget

Vase in the Form of a Bull
Iran

Horse Bit: Human-headed Monster
trampling a Hint
Iran

The Monkey as Painter
Jean-Baptiste-Siméon Chardin

The Monkey as Collector of Antiques
Jean-Baptiste-Siméon Chardin

Landscapes

Landscape with a River and a Cove in the Distance
Joseph Mallord William Turner

121

Souvenir of Mortefontaine
Jean-Baptiste-Camille Corot

Saint Françis Preaching to the Birds
Giotto

Gardens of the Villa d'Este
Jean-Baptiste-Camille Corot

previous page
The Mole,
Seen from the Bacino di San Marco
Canaletto

eft hand page
Jlysses Restores Chryseis to her Father
Claude Lorrain

Pilgrimage to the Isle of Cythera
Jean-Antoine Watteau   129

Magdalena-Bay
François Biard

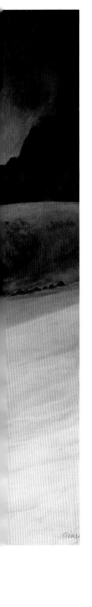

Landscape around Honfleur. Snow
Claude Monet

The Madonna
of Chancellor Rolin
Jan Van Eyck

The Preaching of Saint
Stephen in Jerusalem
Vittore Carpaccio

Portraits

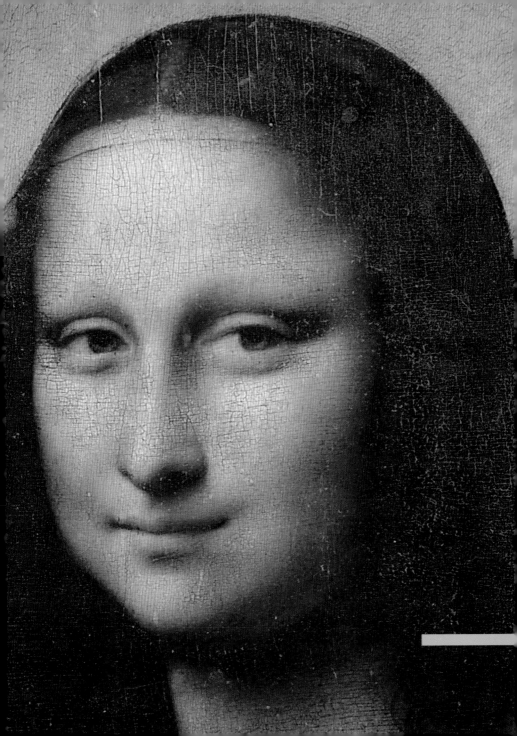

left hand page
The Mona Lisa
Leonardo da Vinci

Head of a Female Figure
Greece

137

Summer
Giuseppe Arcimboldo

Frédéric Chopin
Eugène Delacroix

Head of Aphrodite
Tralles

The Great Odalisque
Jean-Auguste-Dominique Ingres

Sigismondo Pandolfo Malatesta
Piero della Francesca

Head of a Rider
Greece

Self-Portrait
Albrecht Dürer

Venus de Milo
Greece

Sarcophagus of a Couple
Italy

Conversation in a Park
Thomas Gainsborough

The Countess del Carpio,
Marchesa de la Solana
Goya

Mademoiselle Caroline Rivière
Jean-Auguste-Dominique Ingres

previous page
Gabrielle d'Estrées and One of her Sisters
School of Fontainebleau

Portrait of Baldassare Castiglione,
Writer and Diplomat

Raphael

Portrait of a Young Woman
Egypt

Kings, Queens and Great Figures

previous page
The Consecration of Emperor Napoleon
and Coronation of Empress Josephine
Jacques-Louis David

The Abduction of Helen
Guido Reni

King Henri IV receives the Portrait
of his Bride Maria de' Medici
Peter Paul Rubens

The Infanta Mary Marguerite
Diego Velázquez

Charles VII, King of France
Jean Fouquet

1 Charles V
and Jeanne de Bourbon
Île-de-France

2 A Queen
Île-de-France

A King
Île-de-France

3 The Emperor Triumphant
Constantinople

Gudea, Prince of Lagash
Tello

Portrait of Dona Isabel de Requesens
Raphael

left hand page
Louis XIV, King of France
Hyacinthe Rigaud

Charles V's Sceptre
Treasure of Saint-Denis

169

Crown « of Charlemagne »
Martin-Guillaume Biennais

Louis XV's Crown
Treasure of Saint-Denis

Portrait of Fath Ali Shah
Iran

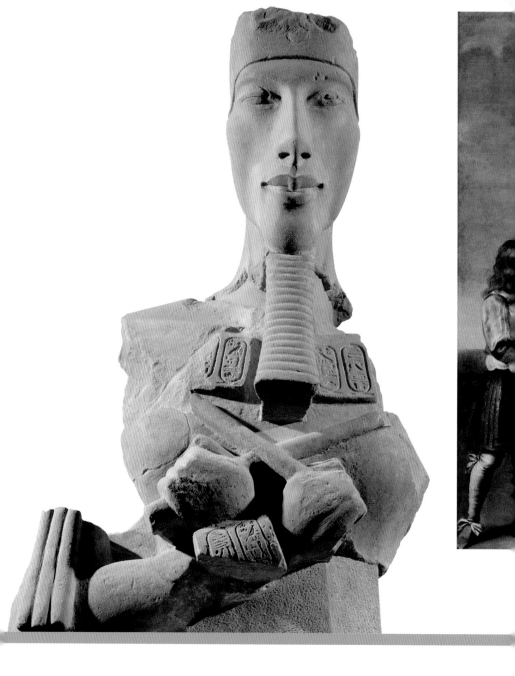

Akhenaton
Egypt

Chancellor Séguier
Charles Le Brun

Princess of Bactria
Mesopotamia

François I, King of France
Jean Clouet

Portrait of John II
the Good, King of France
Paris

right hand page
Portrait of a Young Princess
Pisanello

Charles I, King of England
Antony Van Dyck

Equestrian statue
of Charlemagne
Cathédrale de Metz

Female Boby, probably Nefertiti
Egypt

The Empress Joséphine
Pierre-Paul Prud'hon

Stories

previous page
Ulysse and the Sirens
Italy

The Raft of the Medusa
Théodore Géricault

The Calvary (detail)
Josse Lieferinxe

The Blessed Ranieri Frees the Poor
from a Prison in Florence
Sassetta

The Education of Achilles by the Centaur Chiron
Jean-Baptiste Regnault

Cupid Riding the Centaur
Italy

The Knight, the Maiden and Death
Hans Baldung Grien

The Kidnapping of Europe
Liberale da Verona

Saint Anthony of Padua
and the Miracle of the Mule
Domenico Beccafumi

The Burlesque Comedy
Jean-Baptiste Oudry

Perseus Freeing Andromeda
Joachim Wtewael

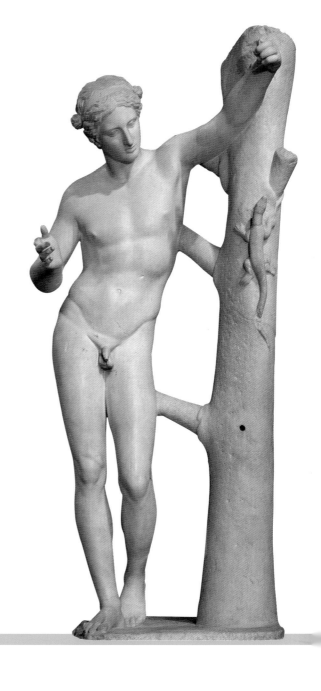

Apollo Sauroctonus
Italy

Krate: fight between Heracles and Antaios
Euphronios (painter) et Euxitheos (potter)

Apollon et Daphne
Giambattista Tiepolo

next page
Defence of the Toll-Gate
at Clichy
Horace Vernet

The Wing Victory
of Samothrace
Greece

Suger Eagle
Treasure of Saint-Denis

The Demon Pazuzu
Mesopotamia

201

Eros and Psyche
Antonio Canova

Psyche and Cupid
François Gérard

205